APERTURE

NUMBER NINETY-TWO
FALL

Aperture, a division of Silver Mountain Foundation, Inc., publishes *Aperture* at Millerton, New York 12546. Officers are Chairman of the Board Shirley C. Burden; President Arthur M. Bullowa; Executive Vice President Michael E. Hoffman; Vice President, Editorial, Carole Kismaric; Secretary Lois Myller, Directors are Robert Anthoine, Arthur M. Bullowa, Shirley C. Burden, Stanley Cohen, Robert Coles, Alan Fern, Robert A. Hauslohner, Michael E. Hoffman, Naomi Rosenblum, Evan H. Turner. Minor White: Editor 1952–1975.

Editorial Director/Publisher, Michael E. Hoffman; Editor, Carole Kismaric; Managing Editor, Mary Wachs; Production Manager, Charles Gershwin; Designer, Wendy Byrne; Circulation Manager, Mary Bilquin; Work-scholar, Steve Dietz. Contributing Editors: Robert Coles, R. H. Cravens, Lloyd Fonvielle, John Gossage, James Baker Hall, Ben Maddow, Anita Ventura Mozley, William Parker, Jed Perl, Joel Snyder, Jonathan Williams.

Cover: Rio Branco, *Untitled*, 1976.

Composition by David E. Seham Assoc., Inc., Metuchen, New Jersey. Black-and-white printing by Meriden Gravure, Inc., Meriden, Connecticut. Contone® color separation and printing by L S Graphic Inc.—D. L. Terwilliger Company, Inc., New York.

Aperture (ISSN 0003-6420) is published quarterly, in February, May, August, and November at Elm Street, Millerton, New York 12546. A subscription for four issues is $32. Second Class Postage is paid at Millerton, New York 12546. Postmaster: send address changes to Aperture, Elm Street, Millerton, New York 12546. A subscription for four issues outside the United States is $36. Because no publication of fine photography can be self-supporting in America, it is hoped that sponsors who wish to help maintain a vital force in photography will become Patrons ($1000), Donors ($500), Friends ($250), Sustaining Subscribers ($150), or Retaining Subscribers ($75). Names of Patrons, Donors, Friends, and Sustaining and Retaining Subscribers will appear in every issue for the duration of their sponsorship. Gifts (the donation less $32 for the subscription to *Aperture*) are tax deductible. Single copies may be purchased for $12.50.

People and Ideas

A promising breeze has been rustling the inner thickets of photography here—new people in new positions, new spaces, plus an emphasis on the rediscovery of early landmark photographs. The Arts Council of Great Britain, not unlike the National Endowment for the Arts in the United States, provides grants to artists and galleries, and is backing major exhibition programs at the Hayward Gallery and the Serpentine Gallery in London as well as providing the services of a tour department. The Arts Council has a new chairman of its Arts Panel—Sir Roy Strong, director of the Victoria and Albert Museum in London. What new directions will the Arts Council pursue under his administration? Strong volunteered recently that photography has a prominent place in his plans. A controversial essay he published a couple of years ago is illuminating. In a critique of *The Story of Modern Art* by Norbert Lynton, Strong wrote: "I'm getting tired of the modern art industry. The public has been brainwashed by decades of the modern-art machine, a complex mechanism whose interests lie in sustaining the myth of modern art. As a result, we are saddled with something that is the consequence of tremendous vested interests by both the people and the institutions whose existence would be undermined if they admitted it was now a myth." The new book was compared unflatteringly with the "absolute clarity of story-line" and panoramic vision of its progenitor *The Story of Art* by E. H. Gombrich.

Anger still flares up in some quarters at Strong's dismissive remarks such as: "On the whole, I feel that there is more than an irritating degree of arrogance about the proponents of modern art, which, in a way, could do with a put-down. It implies an elitism, an exclusion, a perpetual storming of Establishment citadels that eighty years after the event have become more than a boring cliché. In the end even shock becomes a bore." He shrewdly commented on the huge tracts of activity undigested and disregarded by modernist art histories: "In painting, the vitality of the academic stream is of course never once referred to: everyone from Boldini to Munnings is swept into total oblivion. Strange, because the so-called New Realists owe so much to their rediscovery."

It was not all hatchet work. Strong proposed a wholesale restructuring of the history in favor of a horizontal rather than a vertical scheme. By this he meant that the history should identify critical forces (such as the role of exotic cultures in transforming Western art) rather than a tightly packed cluster of isms.

The availability of mass reproduction of the art of all cultures and countries "had an explosive effect on the optic sense." He went on: "One would also have to shift the emphasis from the almost exclusive obsession with painting. Architecture and sculpture barely figure, apart from a wave of the hand to a Bauhaus building or a Henry Moore [sculpture]; the decorative arts not at all, nor photography, nor commercial art. The geographical balance is also solidly Western European. The United States figures only after 1945, and Scandinavia not at all, let alone Latin America, Australia, or Japan."

This autumn the Hayward will mount the first showing of David Hockney's new composite photographs. Hockney calls them "joiners," and they are distinct from his Polaroid composites already published. They are built up from masses—maybe eighty to a hundred—of color photographs (the sort you get from 110 film) joined up to establish a more

O. Winston Link, *Hot Shot East at Iaeger WVA*, 1956

2

or less continuous space. Considering the routine nature of the prints, the quality of the color is ridiculously, impossibly interesting and beautiful. The man is onto something. His show will be paired at the Hayward with the first serious exhibition in recent years of the paintings of Raoul Dufy. To celebrate the surface of life at its most benevolent as both these artists have done seems to be surprisingly difficult; at any rate it is rare. Also booked into the Hayward in the future is a Josef Koudelka retrospective (1984), to be followed by a grand revaluation of Roger Fenton, the truest genius of early British photography, which Valerie Lloyd is preparing in conjunction with the British Art Center at Yale. Strong decided that Fenton fitted into the Victoria and Albert so perfectly that the Hayward was the better place—so that the graphic eloquence of the work could shine without any overlay of Victoriana or of period cliché.

•

Newly installed recently as director of the Olympus Gallery (run by the camera company) is Martin Harrison. He worked as David Bailey's assistant during the 1960s and then became engrossed in Victoriana and stained glass, on which he has published something of a bible for aficionados of the subject. The gallery has moved from its bijou quarters in the Ritz Arcade to an elegantly designed, good-sized space off Regent Street at 24 Princes Street, London W1. It has already shown David Bailey's new architectural series "NW1" (the Camden Town district beside Primrose Hill where Bailey lives) and "Snapshots and Reference Photographs" by Peter Blake, the Pop artist who designed the *Sergeant Pepper* album cover of yesteryear. (Blake is currently enjoying a well-received retrospective at the Tate Gallery.) Harrison is planning also to exhibit a selection of unpublished work by Ralph Eugene Meatyard, about whom he speaks interestingly, and Olympus is publishing the eighty-page catalogue.

•

Sue Davies has been director of The Photographers' Gallery since she opened it—with decisive nerve and determination—in 1971. This year she was awarded the Silver Progress Medal by the Royal Photographic Society (earlier recipients

Ralph Eugene Meatyard, *Untitled*, about 1954–55

include Roger Fenton, P. H. Emerson, and Bill Brandt). A couple of years ago Davies brought in an Oxford graduate, Rupert Martin, as exhibition organizer. Martin has mounted effective survey shows of recent photography in Germany and Britain. The recent exhibition "Floods of Light: Flash Photography 1851–1981" is his most ambitious venture to date.

Martin's interest in the subject began with contemporary photography using flash and led him back to its traditional history in twentieth-century photojournalism, then further back to what he calls the prehistory of the flash before 1887. Flash has two virtues, he writes. It casts light where there is none, and it dissects time, like an early form of fast shutter. The exhibition catalogue includes informative contributions from Valerie Lloyd: *Pioneers and Percursors of Flashlight Photography*, and David Mellor: *The Regime of Flash*.

Mellor argues that the new flashbulb technology of about 1930 "overwhelmed all the genres of news photography, becoming, in its turn, an indispensable portion of the very news event that was being reported. Which is to say that from the early 1930s to the late 1950s the dominant sign of the newsworthy occurrence was the staccato firing of flashbulbs." He writes, with an extravagant poetry of his own: "Flash and the Inception of the To-

talitarian State . . . Hitler's arrival by open car to well-managed media events where beams of light orchestrated the body and the mass: searchlights, torches, mixed with flash. A new variety of the-atrified politics was in formation." He speaks of Hitchcock's *Foreign Correspondent* (1940): "At the beginning of the film a news photographer flashes a central-European Chancellor, and in the moment of the bulb's discharge assassinates him with an automatic pistol held flush with his camera. Violence against the body was already inscribed into the history of flash." One of the many remarkable photographs in the show was an artificial-light masterpiece recently unearthed by The Museum of Modern Art in New York—*Hot Shot East at Iaeger WVA*, 1956, by O. Winston Link.

Like any good show, this one had the effect of leaving a strong afterimage in the mind's eye—like the odd cinematic light in which we walk the streets after seeing a film. The show alerted me to some memory that I could not call to mind until I opened a Sunday newspaper and found a photograph captioned "Three o'clock in the morning, June 18, 1959: Onassis (left) and Meneghini embrace Maria at a party in her honour." From the picture it looked as if Onassis was already on his way to divesting Callas's husband of his diva. The uncomfortable triple embrace was sardonically echoed by the clock. A third man took the flash full in the pupils. A fourth watched, one-eyed, through a chink between the cheek of the star and the forelock of the millionaire. This kind of picture educated our adolescent fantasies of

Joseph Byron, *Woman on Rings, Gymnasium, Dr. Savage's School, New York*, 1889

power, sex, and money in the '50s, punctually every Sunday. I hadn't realized quite how deeply I'd buried such pictures. *The Regime of Flash*, indeed.

•

The general view of British television here is that it is pretty awful but—no false modesty intended—easily the best in the world. Many people believe British radio is also the best in the world but actually something to be proud of. Arts coverage on radio is brisk, well informed, and nightly on the *Kaleidoscope* program on Radio Four, and it is coupled with serious book reviews and the like on Radio Three. But for some reason, "culture" usually goes horribly wrong on the tube. It was thus an unexpected pleasure to watch the BBC series "Master Photographers" recently, a truly exciting series aired at the unbelievably peak hour of 7:30 p.m. Peter Adam of the BBC directed the series and himself interviewed Alfred Eisenstadt, Bill Brandt, Jacques-Henri Lartigue, Andreas Feininger, Ansel Adams, and André Kertész. Adam was extraordinary because, as far as I re-

member, the camera never showed him except from behind the shoulder. This anonymity, together with the simplicity of his questions, was the secret of the success of the programs.

The one on Brandt was a miracle. No one has ever been allowed to tape Bill Brandt before, let alone film him. I've discovered in many talks with Brandt over the last ten years that he and his conversation are addictive. And now we have on film the good sense, inimitable gestures, sparkling light in the clear blue of his eyes, the wonderful room in Kensington unlike and better than almost anywhere else I know, the suprising laugh from deep in his lungs. Brandt simply sat at his round table by the tall windows of his living room, looking at prints and one or two of his books and talking about his pictures, with a question now and again from Peter Adam.

Brandt told how he managed to get his famous portraits of Francis Bacon and Picasso, explaining that *anyone* could have taken good photographs of his *Perfect Parlourmaid* (a fantastic person, he said—no special photographic skills required)."Do you think there is a Decisive Moment in photography?" Chuckle, sparkle of the eyes. Slowly, "It sounds like Cartier-Bresson." Then, firmly and conclusively, "No." More mischievous

chuckles. I suppose I knew most of the stories, but Brandt had new things to say too. Concerning the beginning of his series of nudes in 1945 he revealed that he was interested at the time in the paintings of Balthus. Balthus—as reclusive and enigmatic as Brandt himself, painter of visions of adolescent girls in naked reverie and abandon. We had already tracked Brandt's debt to the *Alice in Wonderland* of Lewis Carroll with its alarming reversals of scale and constriction of decor. Now we had another key piece of the complicated jigsaw of his influence and invention.

•

Photographic activity is widespread. The Whitechapel Art Gallery recently showed a superb double act of paintings by Frida Kahlo, the wife of Diego Rivera, and photographs by Tina Modotti, with a catalogue by Laura Mulvey and Peter Wollen. The Museum of London uncovered and exhibited the photographs of one of the pioneers of the medium and the inventor of the "honey" process, George Shadbolt. In one picture a botanically minded trio sit proudly beside an exotic plant in a mid-Victorian garden of generous dimensions; we are then shown the same site 120 years later—from early Robert Cumming to middle-period Lee Friedlander. It is a neat demonstration of part of Sir Roy Strong's point about the key change in information that has occurred in the modern period: "A centuries-old repertory collapses

Bill Brandt, *Shelter in a Disused Tube Tunnel near Liverpool Street Station*, 1940

like a house of cards to be replaced by no universal language of an educated, cultured class, but instead by a babel of transient public and private mythologies."

The show of the moment is "Landscape in Britain 1850–1950" at the Hayward Gallery, which will subsequently go on tour. As if to flaunt a blatant Post-Modernist intention, the show (selected by Frances Spalding and Ian Jeffrey, author of the new *Photography: A Concise History*) opens with *The Poppy Field*, lovingly if lugubriously painted by Alfred Munnings. The selection charges all over the place: major paintings, little-known ones, etchings, engravings, book jackets, posters, and photographs. Indeed, the photographs prompted a generally sober and thoughtful critic, John McEwen of *The Spectator*, to pronounce that photography was the major landscape medium after 1850. The horizontal restructuring of art history is in full stride.

•

A few days after this letter is dispatched the Queen will be visiting the Victoria and Albert's first new addition in South Kensington since Queen Victoria laid the foundation stone of the Cromwell Road facade in 1899. Among the galleries to be visited are a suite of four devoted—for the first time—to the permanent display of the art of photography.

There are also some interesting developments in photography happening in Scotland, and I shall soon be writing from there.

•

The best quote of the season was Lartigue's answer to the question (on TV): "Is it necessary to be modest to be a good photographer?" To which the maestro replied: "No, I am sure it isn't. I'm modest because I loathe people who aren't."

MARK HAWORTH-BOOTH

Ralph Eugene Meatyard: *Caught Moments – New Viewpoints*, with an introduction by Diane and Christopher Meatyard, is available from the Olympus Gallery, London.

Floods of Light: Flash Photography. 1851–1981, edited by Rupert Martin, is available from The Photographers' Gallery, London.

Who Killed *Camera Arts*?

One day in May editor Jim Hughes and the staff of *Camera Arts* magazine were summoned to a meeting with their publisher. They were told that the July 1983 issue would be their last. *Camera Arts*, the most beautiful and dramatic of the popular photography magazines, a recent winner of the National Magazine Association's Award for Excellence, was to be shut down. *Camera Arts* had lasted two and a half years, twenty-two issues, and was said to be selling 150,000 copies each month. The following announcement appeared in the July issue: "Ziff-Davis is pleased to announce a very important event for the subscribers to *Camera Arts*. After considerable reflection, we have accepted an invitation from the publisher of *American Photographer* to merge with *Camera Arts*."

Camera Arts, owned by Ziff-Davis Publishing Company, which owns some fifty other magazines, has been sold to *American Photographer*, which is owned by CBS. It was, as they say, a corporate decision. *Camera Arts* was not making money. (Neither was Jeanne d'Arc when she was sold to the English.) Maybe it wasn't just a question of money. Motives, even corporate motives, are not always simple. At Ziff-Davis, where pictures are meant to be pretty, *Camera Arts* was beginning to print realistic, disturbing work.

Recently it published Eugene Richards's upsetting essay "Vital Signs," on emergency-room doctors and nurses, and a fourteen-page essay of my pictures made in America over a period of twenty years: photographs of motorcycle gangs; a policeman making an obscene gesture; a collapsed black convict; teenage prostitutes; and naked men in a shower, including what was reported to be the first exposed male genital ever reproduced by Ziff-Davis.

Jim Hughes, who along with Fred Ritchin, the executive editor, and Thomas Ridinger, the art director, brought *Camera Arts* to its preeminent position among the popular photography magazines, has lost magazines the way a good cavalry officer loses horses in battle.

Shortly after he published W. Eugene Smith's essay "Minamata" in *Camera 35* in 1974, that magazine was sold by its owner, the American Express Company. One can argue that Ziff-Davis owned *Camera Arts* and had a right to sell it and close it down. I would argue that we need a popular picture magazine more radical than *Camera Arts* and one not dependent on corporate financing.

The astounding power of corporations and their protection under our present laws have just about wrecked American

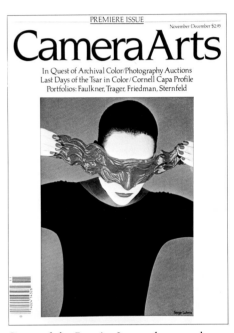

Cover of the Premier Issue; photograph by Serge Lutens

civilization. Our power as individuals has become virtually nonexistent. I spent several years of my life making books of my photographs, all with social and political statements. *The Bikeriders, The Destruction of Lower Manhattan*, and *Conversations with the Dead* (a study of the Texas prison system) were all remaindered after corporations bought the publishing companies that had produced them.

I don't think anyone was trying to censor my books. I don't think they even looked inside them. When CBS bought Holt, Rinehart and Winston they took *Conversations with the Dead* off the shelves. Soon after the second printing, the copies were sold off for a dollar each.

(continued on page 76)

The Proud Pilgrims of Slovakia

Photographs by Markéta Luskačová
Essay by Mark Haworth-Booth

Jacob Riis, an immigrant himself, classified the communities he photographed in New York City late last century. He had this sense of the identity of the Bohemians, newly arrived from what is now the western part of Czechoslovakia: they were the Irish of *Mitteleuropa*. Prague is the capital of that Bohemia, and Markéta Luskačová is one of its citizens—although living now in London. Her photographs were first exhibited at the Theater Behind the Wall in Prague in 1970. A brief text by Josef Topol introduced the exhibit and linked the photographs with the play then being performed, the *Antigone* of Sophocles:

> *People in a file kneeling in a bare land close to the sky, rising, proceeding in song, bending their knees in prayer, rising, and like the chorus from a Greek tragedy, treading their pilgrim's way—to what Delphi?*
>
> *The proud humility of these pilgrims might speak the words of Oedipus as Sophocles had spelt them:* "And Time, my brother, who knew me when I was small, now knows me in my greatness too. I was born thus, nor shall I change any more." *The photographs [Luskačová's] present the spiritual image of man, our contemporary, and of a pilgrimage so rare in our place and time.*

These photographs were taken from 1967 to 1970 and belong to two extensive series. The first is *Pilgrimages*. The second, *Villages*, grew naturally from the first and shows the life and customs of country people with whom the photographer had become friends during pilgrimages to the easternmost part of her country, known as Slovakia. It was in this area, where the rural traditions of the people have held their ground against industrialization, that Markéta Luskacóvá found an immediate spiritual identification.

There are some twelve pilgrimage centers in eastern Slovakia, the greatest of which is Levoca with its renowned Gothic cathedral. The pilgrimages are part of the Marian cult strong in the region. Four to five thousand people, primarily Roman Catholic, attend the festival at Levoca on the fourth of July, with lesser festivals scattered over the following two months.

Luskačová would travel the 600 kilometers east from Prague to join the pilgrimage on a Thursday or Friday. The chief service would be on Sunday, but smaller services would be held late into Saturday evening and begin again at first light. Afterward, she would travel back to Prague, process and print photographs to give to pilgrims she knew, and set out again on the Thursday. This cycle was maintained over the eight to ten weeks of the summer pilgrimages.

One photograph shows Katarina, a pilgrim, seated in her house (page 19); another (page 18) shows her icon-hung "best" room. Katarina was a friend the photographer made in her third year of photographing the pilgrimages. She lived in a mountain village that retained much of its eighteenth-century, preindustrial character, as the land was poor and there was no farm co-operative. Perhaps its peasant traditions stretched much further back than that. Katarina once explained to the village priest how her friend Markéta began to photograph their life: "She was photographing us on a pilgrimage, and then she brought us pictures, and because she brought us pictures, we said, 'Come on girl, have a meal with us.' And she said, 'Could I come to your village?,' and we said, 'Yes, you can come to our village.' And she came to the village, and we gave her a meal!"

The photographer remembers Katarina looking up from her bible one day and saying: "The world used to be much more beautiful. . . . A place where angels used to tread."

The community was bound together by mutual help and obligation. A tally was kept of the time neighbors and relations owed each other. Each day or half day was carefully recorded and had to be returned. Failure to make good the owed time resulted in loss of standing. At the end of each harvest Katarina was able to say with pride: "All my time debts are paid, I owe no one any time."

One day in Prague the photographer received a telegram. Katarina's mother had died. Could she come to the funeral and would she photograph it? It was considered proper for a person to be prepared for death after the age of fifty, with funeral clothes and holy candles arranged in readiness in a chest. In contrast to attitudes in modern society, death was not experienced as a violent and arbitrary intrusion into life but was anticipated and accepted as the natural conclusion of living. The curate would compose a chant for the dead person, in which the departed says goodbye to each relation and neighbor, each by name and in strictly observed order. The photographer found that she herself was remembered and was bade goodbye in the chant.

In the village a number of old customs were observed by the priest, such as blessing each house at Christmas. There was also the Ceremony of the Cape. This Easter ritual concerned a sacred cape painted with a crucifixion. On Good Friday the cape would be ceremoniously carried in procession three times around the church. Then it would be placed in a grave or shrine inside the church. On Easter Sunday the cape would be taken up from the grave or shrine and again carried in procession three times around the church. Unlike a painted panel or a cross, the cape assumed different forms responsive to its ritual passage, as it was held, carried, and kissed.

It is not easy to decide whether to write about the culture represented in the photographs in the past or present tense. There is a cooperative in the village now. Small things are changing—modern brushed cottons replace the customary materials of dress, whose cut and decoration conveyed a sense of local tradition and a style of proud deportment. By some the old ways are now being seen as primitive, as belonging to an age now considered as pre-prosperous and, therefore, somehow preposterous. Already the two series of photographs have acquired a documentary quality that may be unrepeatable.

While the subjects of the photographs belong to a period we may regard as archaic, the pictures inevitably reflect an awareness of contemporary external influence. Their style is fully accounted for by books likely to have been available to the photographer in Prague—Henri Cartier-Bresson's and William Klein's Moscow books, the first for its vocabulary of small-camera framing, the second for its graphic freedom. Undoubtedly, the photographer had ready access to the examples of Josef Sudek and Josef Koudelka.

There is, though, a more persistent reason for including the photographs in our modern consciousness, expressed in the memorable description of a group of peasants from Central Europe displaced to a railway station in the Ukraine during the Second World War, written by Czeslaw Milosz in *The Captive Mind*:

In my wanderings at the beginning of the Second World War, I happened to find myself, for a very short while, in the Soviet Union. I was waiting for a train at a station in one of the large cities of the Ukraine. It was a gigantic station. Its walls were hung with portraits and banners of inexpressible ugliness. A dense crowd dressed in sheepskin coats, uniforms, fur caps, and woolen kerchiefs filled every available space and tracked thick mud over the tiled floor. The marble stairs were covered with sleeping beggars, their bare legs sticking out of their tatters despite the fact that it was freezing. Over them loudspeakers shouted propaganda slogans. As I was passing through the station I suddenly stopped and looked. A peasant family—husband and wife and two children—had settled

down by the wall. They were sitting on baskets and bundles. The wife was feeding the younger child; the husband, who had a dark, wrinkled face and a black, drooping mustache was pouring tea out of a kettle into a cup for the older boy. They were whispering to each other in Polish. I gazed at them until I felt moved to the point of tears. What had stopped my steps so suddenly and touched me so profoundly was their difference. *This was a human group, an island in a crowd that lacked something proper to humble, ordinary human life. The gesture of a hand pouring tea, the careful, delicate handing of the cup to the child, the worried words I guessed from the movement of their lips, their isolation, their privacy in the midst of the crowd—that is what moved me. For a moment, then, I understood something that quickly slipped from my grasp.*

Polish peasants were certainly far from the summits of civilization. It is possible that the family I saw was illiterate. My friend would have called them graceless, smelly imbeciles who had to be taught to think. Still, precious seeds of humanity were preserved in them, or in the Baltic people, or in the Czechs because they had not yet been subjected to the scientific treatment of Monsieur Homais. It may well be that the fondness with which Baltic women tended their little gardens, the superstition of Polish women gathering herbs to make charms, the custom of setting an empty place for a traveler on Christmas Eve betoken inherent good that can be developed. In the circles in which my friend lives, to call man a mystery is to insult him. They have set out to carve a new man much as a sculptor carves his statue out of a block of stone, by chipping away what is unwanted. I think they are wrong, that their knowledge in all its perfection is insufficient, and their power over life and death is usurped.

More recently there is John Berger's literary project on the peasantry of Western Europe, of which *Pig Earth* is the first work. Berger states that "within a century there may be no more peasants. In Western Europe, if the plans work out as the economic planners have foreseen, there will be no more peasants within twenty-five years. . . . The remarkable continuity of peasant experience and the peasant view of the world acquires, as it is threatened with extinction, an unprecedented and unexpected urgency."

Markéta Luskačová made these photographs from 1967 to 1970 in Slovakia, in eastern Czechoslovakia.

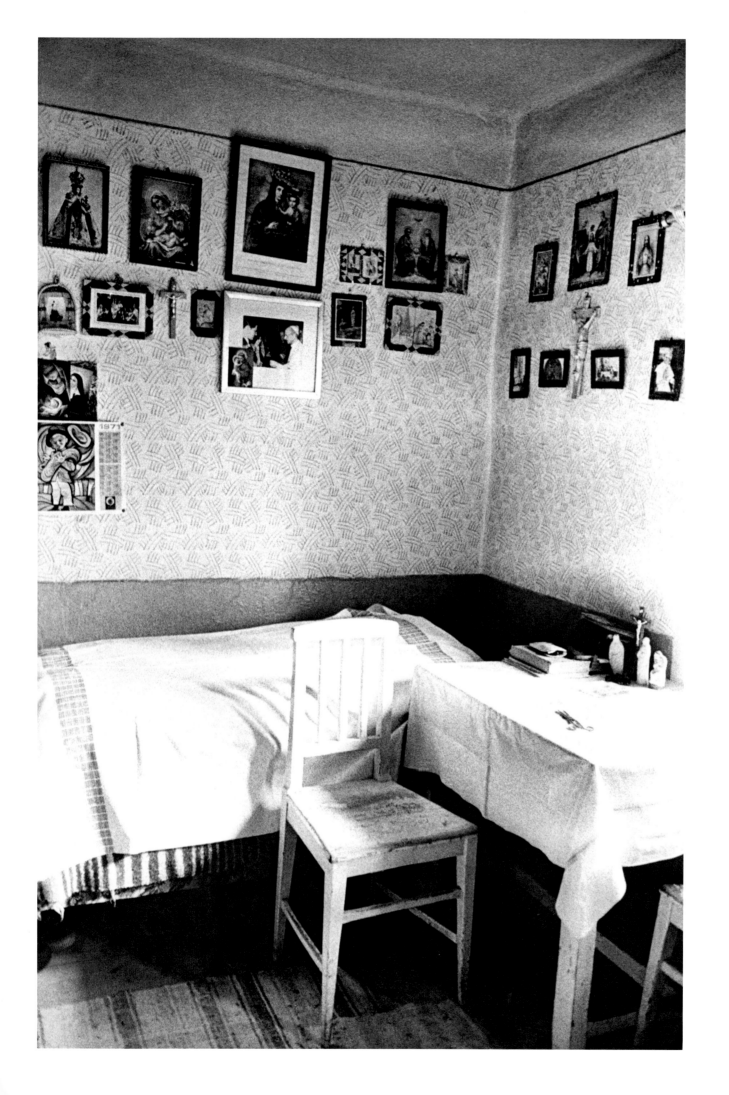

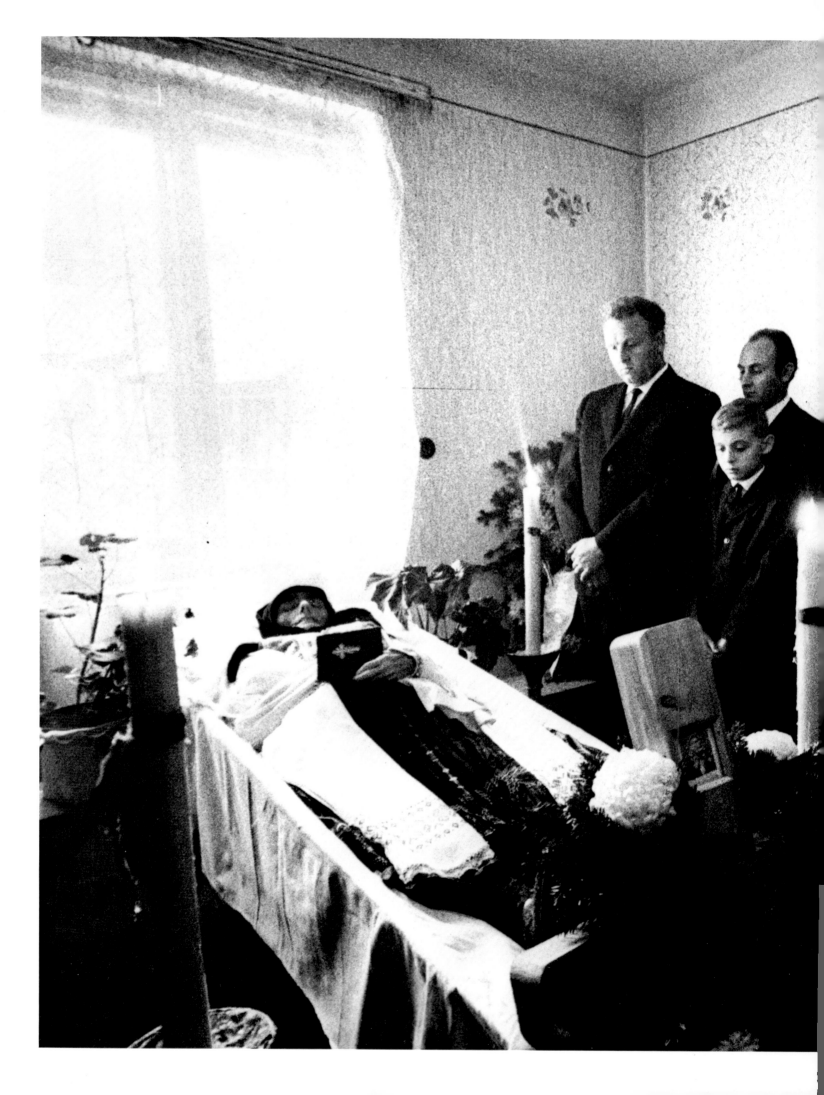

Tears and Misunderstanding

By Ben Maddow

The persistent problem in photography is how to look at it.

In 1916, at the age of twenty-six, Paul Strand went to Alfred Stieglitz, whom he had visited many times before, with a splendid new series of photographs that included a number of portraits of ordinary people. They had been taken by stealth on the streets of New York with a fake brass-bound lens attached to his reflex. They remain among the very greatest American photographs. But do we see them properly?

There is no doubt of Strand's social conscience; after all, he was a pupil of Lewis Hine's. But in this youthful series, he went beyond the assignments of Jacob Riis and Hine and penetrated to a deeper level. His work that year rivals even Rembrandt in its fearless insight. The *Blind Woman* is the most celebrated; it appears in Helmut and Alison Gernsheim's *The History of Photography*, in Beaumont Newhall's *The History of Photography*, and in many other anthologies. The woman, with a cast in one eye, is unique, powerful within herself, with a face as marked and enduring as a boulder facing the sea. "I like," said Strand, "to photograph people who have strength and dignity in their faces. Whatever life has done to them, it hasn't destroyed them."

But do we see this woman as Strand saw her? We are deceived because she wears a sign around her neck: BLIND, and we give her the automatic, easy pity that such a title—for that's what it really is—provokes. Tears rise agreeably to our eyes, and we respond with the clouded vision of our sentimentality. The fact is, she's not a beggar: she's a licensed newspaper vendor on Lexington Avenue at 34th Street. If we change that sign to a Chinese character or, better yet, put our hand over it, the woman changes, too. We see more directly into her spirit; she is obdurate and enduring, patient, and a bit unpleasant. The best proof of our misapprehension is the lesser fame of the other portraits taken in the same season; in particular the greatest of the series, a man in a derby hat. Here is Paul Strand at one of the many peaks of his career: complex truth, not without compassion, but without the stoic nobility that he required later on. Strand was an inheritor of the American populist tradition, as old as Andrew Jackson, that sees each particular person as a symbol of The People. The whole calendar of his later portraits, though brilliant and true, is inferior to the early New York series because Strand insisted that his subjects face the camera with the frontal, stubborn dignity that was his own. We might almost say that the photographs are a series of self-portraits.

Paul Strand, *Blind Woman, New York*, 1916

Alfred Stieglitz, *The Steerage*, 1907

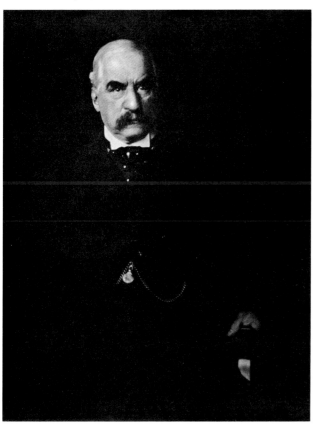

Edward Steichen, *J. P. Morgan, New York*, 1903

His mentor, Stieglitz, had no such dogmatic message for the world. Yet his most famous photograph, reproduced in all the standard histories, is clouded by just such a social misunderstanding. By its very name, *The Steerage*, it invokes our sympathy for the immigrants to America; many were our grandparents who were conveyed, it's true, crowded, hungry, and seasick, on the lowest deck. Should we not pity and admire them? Certainly; except that the people in Stieglitz's print were not immigrants at all: they were going the other way, along with the photographer, to the port of Bremen in Germany. Does this knowledge destroy the photograph? Does it remain a pure exercise in lines and tones? No. The truth is more complicated.

Stieglitz has carefully described his own motivation: "I saw shapes related to one another"—the white lozenge of the gangplank cutting the frame in two; the heavy mast leaning left from top to bottom; the circular shape of the straw hat as the fulcrum of the upper half, balancing the circle of the windlass in the lower left. But that wasn't the whole story. Stieglitz hated the people with whom he traveled in first class; and this simple antibourgeois feeling drew him outdoors, where he could peer into the lower depths: "This seemingly new vision that held me—people, the common people, the feeling of ship and ocean and sky and the feeling of release that I was away from the mob called the rich—Rembrandt came into my mind and I wondered would he have felt as I was feeling." But notice that he spoke of "people," not of any specific person. Indeed, it is hard to see real individuals down there; their faces don't matter. The photograph has become merely an illustration, and perhaps that was Stieglitz's fault as well as our own.

Here is the root of our misunderstanding: we make symbols out of collective facts. We love or hate or are indifferent to whole classes of persons instead of a particular man or woman. The profusion of symbolic thinking in photography can only be compared to the worst excesses of popular painting of the nineteenth and early twentieth centuries. We can only deepen our response to photographs by burning away the fog of shallow reference. We must try to touch a deeper meaning, more personal, nonverbal, an emotion too precise to have a name.

A classic misunderstanding still clouds Edward Steichen's well-known portrait of J. P. Morgan. We read it as "Morgan the Pirate" and enjoy the symbolic dagger in his hand. But Steichen wrote: "Over the years people have referred to the insight into Morgan's real character that I showed by photographing him with a dagger in his hand. But this was their own fanciful interpretation of Morgan's firmly grasping the arm of the chair." There's another contemporary photograph of Morgan in which a press agent put a midget on his lap. When my father saw this image on the front page of a New Jersey newspaper, he said, "Aha! Capitalism!" We disregard what actually happened and project our feelings onto the subject, thus preventing ourselves from seeing the true, complicated, ferocious energy of the man. We've made a perfectly fine portrait into an abstraction.

A famous case in point is Dorothea Lange's beautiful *Migrant Mother*. Here we are fooled by perfectly correct inferences: the subject is thin, perhaps hungry, certainly poor, and obviously dead tired. But her nobility in the face of suffering is an artifact of our social history. We know she was photographed in the 1930s, during the Depression, that she was living in a tent with three small children. We should not erase this knowledge, even if we could. What we must do is not allow it to sentimentalize the woman, to show her as *Migrant Mother* instead of a particular woman. So we pervert the image itself: we read the two older children's hidden faces as mourning. More likely they were simply shy and would a moment later grin and giggle at the camera. The baby in the mother's arms is simply asleep; but swept up in our easy emotion, we read the baby as miserable. All the visual information has been biased by our sympathy, and we don't see the image for what it is. The particular person has disappeared in a mist of lazy generality.

The woman in the photograph is still alive today, but she takes little pleasure in it: "I never got one red cent." Lange herself had conflicting thoughts about this work. She complained, "I'm not a one-shot artist," but she came to enjoy the fame anyhow. Some of Dorothea Lange's best work has escaped a shallow fame, particularly her portrait of a young female cotton picker with a cloth shading her head, photographed in Arizona in 1941. In this portrait we see a real person, not merely a page of history.

Our experience of the last hundred and fifty years has given excessive importance to the visual world, but truth is by no means self-evident; the dominion of self can be tyrannical, and our prejudice can obscure the plainest image.

The worst deceptions are invented by photographers of the second rank. Edward Curtis, along with the rest of us, was the victim of an American paradox. An aggressive white puritan people, armed with guns and smallpox, faced an aggressive puritan people with red skin. The first declared the second to be plainly barbaric and tricky, and at the same time childlike, picturesque, and noble. James Fenimore Cooper, Henry Wadsworth Longfellow, and Currier and Ives all hankered after a golden age—pure and primitive man living in pure and primitive nature, Adam and Eve before the apple. We sent the army to destroy their paradise, never worrying about the contradiction; we dispossessed the wild man when he would go or killed him when he would not. We aggrandized and destroyed him at the same time; we novelized and poetized and painted and photographed him as the noble remnant of a vanished race; fortunately, the stubborn varmint refused to disappear. With numerous examples of real Indians living in every state of the union, we managed to enshrine, as late as the 1960s, the same false Indian, complete with fringes and headband.

The immense labor of Curtis (forty thousand plates, of which twenty-two hundred were published) was no more than a rhetorical and melancholy theater. By the time he was at work

Dorothea Lange, *Migrant Mother, Nipomo, California*, 1936

Edward Curtis, *Cheyenne, The Story of the Washita*, 1927

(1899-1927), Indians ate white flour and pork belly, wore blue jeans, felt hats, and long white cotton dresses, and drove buggies and Model-T Fords. Curtis would have none of this confusion; he borrowed feathers and fringed leather shirts and abalone nose rings and even dark wigs to put on Indians who had intermarried with whites for generations. He constructed scenes and portraits of a noble, serene, proud life that no longer existed—if it ever had.

We still find it hard to realize that American Indians were a varied lot. Some were nomads, some steadfast village farmers. Indeed, they were very much persons like ourselves. Certainly they had their full share of human ills: the prestige and the force of property, political and sexual tyranny, and they murdered their fellow Indians in the very best European tradition.

Honest photography of the American Indian is rare. Still, there were honest men such as Adam Vroman, working at largely the same period as Curtis, who were careful to stage nothing and resurrect nothing. Vroman was so trusted by the Hopis that they let him photograph down in the kivas themselves and record the ceremonial dressing of the snake priests just as it happened. His everyday photographs show the blue jeans and the suspenders as well as the turquoise-and-silver belts. Yet there are portraits in the elephant folios of Curtis where the individuals, beadwork and all, reveal a deeper quality, moving and even exalted. The man was sensitive; the fault in the perception is ours as much as his.

Thus we who enjoy the photograph bring it into our own theater of the subconscious and manage only too often to distort what the artist has plainly given us. Or perhaps not so plainly: Edward Weston's peppers are a troubling case. Weston was an obsessed shopper in the supermarket of the visual, and he made his studies of squash, cabbage, cauliflower, and artichoke in the search for a platonic ideal—or so he supposed. But was he right? He stated, in his characteristically firm style, that the pepper was "completely outside subject matter. It has no psychological attributes, no human emotions are aroused: this new pepper takes one beyond the world we know in the conscious mind. [It takes] one into an inner reality—the absolute—with a clear understanding, a mystic revealment."

Yet the famous *Excusado*, which, knowing perfectly well that it is a porcelain toilet in a Mexican house, we force ourselves to consider an abstract form in the tradition of Duchamp's urinal of 1913, was not all that disembodied in Edward Weston's mind. Depressed and disturbed, he wrote to his friend John Hagemeyer that it represented his true state of mind. Can we disregard such an autobiographical fact?

When he sent some of these vegetable prints to Tina Modotti, his former mistress, she declared them obviously erotic. So they are, too obviously so, and we should distrust the obvious, because that's the very plane on which our preconceptions operate. What distorts our view of photographic prints is a secret fear of reality concealed by our extraordinary and useful human ability to symbolize. Apes might find these peppers simply edible or, if told that they were erotic, might find them disgusting for their lack of hair.

Is every smoothly rounded or smoothly indented surface—animal or fruit or stone—to be called erotic? If so, most of the world would be saturated with sculptural lust, and perhaps it is, in some metaphysical sense. Isn't it simpler and even truer to say that the shapes of naked human love are examples of the general curves in which nature chooses to grow? I have in my possession the drawing of a family of luscious and erotic curves; they are in fact "an isometric view of Antarctica depicting the . . . depression of the surface . . . under the ice load." Maybe Edward Weston was right about his own work, after all: to see peppers as erotic may be just a form of aesthetic kitsch—a humbling admission for critics like us.

It's better to disregard nothing, neither the artist's illusions and feelings nor our own. Notice the hidden axiom that art, whatever else it is in our culture, is communication—a message from the creator to the viewer. Therefore, we have a right to examine the assumptions on both sides until we can look at a photographic print a little more truly each time we see it. Luckily, art is serene and patient and will accompany us through the labyrinth of all our miscalculations.

Edward Weston was a remarkably conscious artist. His idea, though borrowed from the fashionable philosophers of his time, helps us to see the values of his work. In the case of Eugène Atget, we have a different sort of problem. We have no certain idea of how he viewed his own images. He was the very ideal of the modest craftsman. We wonder what he thought when the Surrealists discovered in a certain few of his images the dreaming truth they had sought in tribal art, in the drawings of children, in the art of schizophrenics. The New York gallery of Julien Levy, one of the earliest to hang Surrealist works, exhibited Atget in 1932 along with Salvador Dali, Max Ernst, Man Ray, and Joseph Cornell. Atget's photographs were reproduced, poorly, in the early issues of ephemeral Surrealist magazines—but so were the works of "Elen" Levitt, misspelled and misinterpreted. The French Surrealists never saw the whole body of Atget's work. In fact, they had little interest in photography as such. Those famous ghostly corsets in a Parisian window had for them the tranced sexuality they longed to achieve.

Atget's work, seen in bulk, is solidly in the French graphic tradition. France preferred straight photography from the very start. Atget photographed much the same material as his predecessors Adolf Braun and Charles Nègre. The latter's careful studies of Chartres Cathedral and of Parisian marketplaces, and even his photograph of an organ grinder and two children, done in 1852 (or perhaps earlier), could fit quite easily into Atget's work, but the last is inferior to Atget's picture of the organ grinder and a child singer—here Atget moves away from simple objectivity.

Eugène Atget, *Boulevard de Strassbourg*, 1912

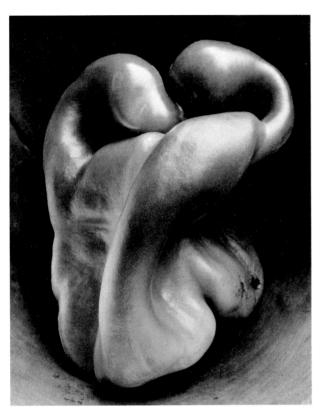

Edward Weston, *Pepper No. 30*, 1930

Walker Evans, *Atlanta, Georgia*, 1936

Atget, we know, had to make a living. He sold his prints and often his negatives, too, not merely to artists (Utrillo was his best customer) but to various French government bureaus. In fact, he would sell the same photograph to two different departments, especially those that were interested in the look and history of Paris and its suburbs. There is no doubt that, on occasion, his photographs are far more than simple documents. Partly it's the material itself: the architecture of trees, the patterns in the dark glass of storefronts, the more complex texture of a ragpicker's hut decorated to the point of madness. Though Atget photographed many street scenes with people—a Punch and Judy show, the wheel of chance at a street fair—they are, to my mind, less compelling. The best studies have the melancholy romanticism of quiet water, early streets, and corroded stone.

Things were the key to Atget's obsession. In an earlier century he would have been an artist devoted to painting genre, the familiar and the curious. We misread Atget if we see in his work either the secret, mysterious power of the naïve or the thankless labor of humble, unknown genius. He was what most photographers were and many still are—craftsmen who are often capable of very fine work within a strict tradition, like Shaker carpenters or circus acrobats or television writers.

Now we must disentangle the work of a rather more complicated artist, Walker Evans, through an image famous and misunderstood on three levels. The lowest is a visual pun: the heavily shaded eyes of Carole Lombard echo the arches of the houses above them. Then there is the ironic contrast: Hollywood glamour superimposed on the decrepit homes of the Depression. Finally, there is a comment on the shallow amusements of the people who live in these identical houses. It is certainly not the first print to be read in this superficial way, but it is famous enough to be the ancestor of thousands more, all of them making no more than the easy connection between two accidental elements. In the same category are Weegee's bag lady scowling at opera patrons; the Robert Doisneau joke of a woman not looking at the nude back of a painting in a shopwindow—much more famous than the far more interesting and troubling Doisneau of *Un Consommateur* over his wine; and Henri Cartier-Bresson's Balinese woman, with full young breasts, brushing past an old lady with withered dugs; we can think of dozens more, some, unfortunately, our favorite prints.

I believe Walker Evans's intent was a lot deeper than visual jokes. He was an intellectual aristocrat: social observation, not social compassion, was part of his nature. But like many other American artists of his time, he was fascinated by the gauche forms of popular art. He collected illustrated postcards for the crudity of their color, and his interest expanded logically into all sorts of Americana—houses, signs, and faces. His sophisticated interest in the small-town southern and middle-American scene has been sadly debased; we have an abundance these days of pictures of dull parking lots and empty sidewalks.

Evans was never dull; his prints have an extraordinary energy from edge to edge. They play with inside and outside. He is interested in the architecture of surface and has photographed a whole series of concave, somber rooms whose space is defined by the complex objects they contain.

To see these things in Evans, particularly in the interiors, we must study his photographs at length. They go past mere tricks, and beyond Evans's occasional condescension. They resemble novellas in the compressed riches of fact and memory. But it is the Lombard photograph that is liked, reproduced, and imitated—and misunderstood—and to which we happily give our half second of spurious excitement. That's our fault again, not Evans's.

We look at photographs too quickly. Partly it's their normal size: usually we can hold them between our hands and scan them without moving our heads. Partly it's a lazy habit: we glance at pictures as if into a passing window. In too many cases, they are constructed so that two seconds is all the time they need to be understood. Rapid composition has produced rapid viewing, although this is not a necessary correlation. We can learn to see with amazing speed, particularly in the moving drama of a city street; something exposed at 1/125 of a second can still produce a complex photograph.

That is clearly true for most of Cartier-Bresson's work. He carried his Leica under his arm wherever he walked, and his vision was rapacious, swift as a bird. Yet his work, subtle and very often profound, is misunderstood as simply a miraculous dissection by the knife of time.

The man leaping into what looks like a deep pond has been read by most of us as a nice visual joke: a fully clothed man jumping into an illusory lake. It is not this photograph, however, but imitations of the famous leap over shallow water that have damaged a generation of photographers. It is very easy to produce the visual trick, the pun of temporary collocation; it enables one to shoot blindly (indeed, a blindfold photographer could do it as well, maybe better), and go back to the darkroom to pick one happy joke out of a sheet of disorganized proofs. What we get, sometimes, is not all bad. It may be a cynical revelation, but rarely is it a work of art.

Jokes are not very often Cartier-Bresson's intent. He looked through a hole in a fence behind the Saint-Lazare station in Paris and photographed what he saw. He apologized for the faulty composition—the edge of the hole obstructed the left side of the visual field—because he was interested in far more than tricks of amusement. In a personal letter Cartier-Bresson wrote, "For me I think there is ugliness only when a thing is disorganized."

He was most influenced, not by photographers, but by living French painters, many of whom he admired and photographed. Georges Braque, Henri Matisse, Pierre Bonnard, all followed the long French tradition of strong construction: vision under control of the intellect; energy constrained within a balance of

Henri Cartier-Bresson, *Behind the Saint-Lazare station*, Paris, 1932

Ansel Adams, *Moonrise, Hernandez, New Mexico*, 1941

boundaries. At the same time, Cartier-Bresson's social and aesthetic bias was that of the Surrealists: Louis Aragon was his friend, André Lhote his early teacher. Their dogma was anti-bourgeois. The Surrealists were in love with the grace of the accidental, of children posing at a broken wall, of the queer, unequal light reflected from the eyes of a swarthy man.

Organization, the grip of choice and reason on the shifting objects of reality, was Cartier-Bresson's method. His delicate sense of balance remained at the service of a satiric lyricism. His photograph of a French family picnicking on the banks of the Seine, a vignette almost redolent of comfortable fat, garlic, and the humble river breeze, was actually commissioned by a left-wing weekly to demonstrate the possibilities of a shorter workday. Compare it with Georges Seurat's lyric and pensive *Sunday Afternoon* on the banks of a river. How sharp is the edge of Cartier-Bresson's intelligence! In his preface to *The Decisive Moment*, he described his search for "one moment at which the elements in motion are in balance. Photography must seize upon this moment and hold immobile the equilibrium of it." With these words he teaches us not only how to make but how to look at his particular discoveries in photography.

Now at last I am forced to confront, with some cowardice, Ansel Adams's extraordinary *Moonrise over Hernandez*. Certainly it is a picturesque, romantic, and splendid scene; it is the very essence of the prize postcard, the photograph we wish we had taken had we not been too lazy or too tired to get out of the car. How sweetly astonishing are the deeply filtered sky, as black as outer space, and the brilliant late-afternoon light on the tombstone, the classic adobe church, the quaint village, the snow on the distant range—and then finally, incredibly, not the sun but the daylight moon rising from under a long pillow of cloud. It is not the organization of the photograph that makes so strong an appeal but the raw ingredients, most especially that amazing moon. Substitute any other round object—the sun, perhaps, or even a balloon—and the whole piece falls apart.

The filter through which we see this landscape is almost inescapable. Our taste in landscape, I think, is especially debased. That's not Ansel Adams's fault. He has made a great quota, not all that recognized, of fine, keenly observed, beautifully organized photographs: the woman behind the screen door in the small town of Independence, California; the solitary rock capped with snow. What does he say about his own work? "I believe in growing things, and in the things that have grown and died magnificently. I believe in people, in the simpler aspects of human life, in the relation of man to nature. I believe man must be free, both in spirit and society, that he must build strength into himself, affirming the enormous beauty of the world."

Adams is an intellectual, aware of the pitfalls and the opportunities in wild landscape—the special values, the infinite gradations of tone, for example, that all photography gratefully borrows from reality. But nature is infinitely corruptible, too. Sunsets and rainbows are marvelous in fact, but they can be cloying in a photograph. Adams himself has abjured the obvious, yet he has made prints that allow us to look superficially, to feel a sentimental splendor, and little else.

We are up against a peculiar contradiction. Does this love of nature pervert nature? At the same time, can a photographer make pictures at all without some emotion behind the lens? Can an automaton (say, a videotape recorder in a bank, registering entrances and exits) generate works of art? It's possible but discomforting; it would depend on the cold idiocy of chance. Does the photographer have to love the subject? Yes, provided love is sharpened by wisdom; but can a photographer have too much knowledge? Does it matter that the composition of two of the most famous Civil War photographs—of a sharpshooter dead in his stone nest, of distorted corpses on the battlefield at Antietam—was manipulated by the photographer(s), that these dead men were dragged up and rearranged for the camera? Probably not.

The last known photograph of Abraham Lincoln with all its limitations of shallow focus and cracked plate still moves us very deeply. But suppose we didn't know that Alexander Gardner had posed Lincoln after the surrender at Appomatox and four days before John Wilkes Booth fired his one-shot derringer into the back of that head? Worse yet, suppose we're Chinese and don't know Lincoln from any other Big Nose. Can the photograph be seen simply as the portrait of a kindly middle-aged man who has lived through bitterness, guilt, and anxiety and looked at the truth of his life with some acceptance? I think so. I also think that the great store of personal memory can enlighten our experience. The complex world that is in the photograph can be matched to a similar world inside ourselves. This is far less true of the other graphic arts, which have cut their umbilical cords to reality. Photography is still nourished by this great mother.

There is no contradiction here. The tears and misunderstanding with which we obscure certain great photographs from ourselves spring from a common fallacy. We substitute an easy symbol for the complexity of the specific. It's natural to enjoy wit and skill in superficial work. This is a nice part of life, and not to be wholly misprised.

Yet the criteria for the greatest photographs remain the same as they were 150 years ago: the refinement of tonality, which is one to one, almost, with nature; and strong construction within the borders of the frame. Even when these are neglected, a beautiful photograph retains something less definable: a voyeurist intensity of vision, an appetite for the miscellaneousness of the universe, on which the artist struggles to impose a fragile order. It is this abnormal passion that photography shares with the arts of literature, mathematics, and science as one of the glories of the mind. Mere contraptions, manipulations, tricks, coincidences, and mock playlets will not do. The uniqueness of persons, the inexhaustible drama of the visual world—these are the only fit subjects for genius.

Philipp Scholz Rittermann: Moonlighting

Text by Mary Wachs

Ask about his night pieces and Philipp Scholz Rittermann will answer that he arrived at them purely by chance. He was wholesaling tea for a German concern at the time. It was 1980. Driving back and forth across West Germany he found himself searching out the commercial zones that lie at the outskirts of cities. At night, after the close of business, he would return to them, as if to a secret lover. The attraction was magnetic. Some months later, when the infatuation died down, he began to understand what had so drawn him—he'd wanted to meet the giant.

While most of us respond with reservation toward the industry around us, Rittermann transforms his ambivalence into occasions for photographs. He says, "I can't deny industry is a part of me," though for many years he futilely attempted to do just that. "I love taking the motorway at 100 miles per hour. But I'm disturbed that the tree is cut down to make room for it." The tension of this attitude informs the pictures Rittermann makes: while the structural clarity and force of industrial objects clearly appeal to him, his photographs pack a resounding caution against mechanized living.

"I don't want to tell a specific story," he explains. "I want to free the viewer of as many associations as possible. Our drive to label everything disallows for the possibility of mystery. 'Science is spoiling my dinner,' someone said. Not science itself, but our process of disenchanting things, picking apart what it takes to fall in love, for instance."

During his night walks Rittermann divines what Keats knew as "negative capability"—as he is compelled toward uncertainty, mystery, and doubt, without any irritable reaching after fact or reason. The night becomes a way-station where one pauses to renew, to learn again how to dream. It occurs to the photographer that we have become alien to the night within ourselves.

"Dusk, dawn, and evening have always been the time for irrational thought and feeling, sometimes scary, often comforting—never neutral. At night our everyday surroundings become strongly ambiguous." In Rittermann's pictures we are thrown back and forth across a whole range of "stage sets" on which we can allow our imagination to soar. The scene, the mood is never indifferent—lyrical one moment, and the next eerie; by turns strange and familiar. The big, black night, once full of phantoms, quiets down.

"While I'm exposing the film—from one half hour to as long as two hours—there is lots of time to wander around and soak up the mood. There are any number of things happening in the sky, on the ground, and inside myself. The balance between ease and fear is often very delicate and can be completely disrupted by the mere snapping of a twig beyond the pool of light somewhere close by. There is a direct correlation between darkness and suspicion when I encounter other people. The darker and dingier the area, the wider the distance between us when we pass each other. And when it's snowing and there is light everywhere, very friendly and often interesting conversations ensue."

For the most part there are no human forms across this *Abendländische Kultur* ("evening-land culture"); as viewers we assume the narrative role, our participation enhanced by the absence of actors who would work for us. Peering across the vacant lot, *we* round the corner by the soccer field (page 38). The sound of pebbles underfoot is suddenly, mysteriously heard.

Occasionally, Rittermann poses in his photographs, but very far from the camera—a visitor passing through. Sometimes one glimpses a semitranslucent blurred form, revealing itself to us only after we are familiar with the picture. We see in the figure time passing as it moves through exposure time and is obliterated by its own haste.

At night, when our perceptions are free of mundane associations, the prosaic becomes chimerical. Entering territory that during the day would forbid us, as in a dairy production plant (page 40), we find our own involvement overcomes the sterile, organized, tidy, precise aura of this place. The greenhouse (page 40) looks about to ascend into outer space. In a railway picture (page 41) we easily travel beyond our customary destination. One viewer has told Rittermann he sees the concentration camp of his childhood in the photograph; for another, his child's model train is evoked. Rittermann observes that during the day the common purpose of a factory is in the foreground. But in his pictures the day retires. We dare to engage the immensity of our inner being.

We build industry on the edges of civilization when we can, benefiting from it as we deny its existence. In German there is a word for what in English we know as industrial dumps: they call them *entsorgung*—connoting "taking away worry." Literally, the word means "making inactive." It is part of the magic of these pictures that this transitional territory, a no-man's land built between cities and responsible to none, renders us wholly accountable to ourselves. A lot of *sorgung* is a lot of worry, but in Rittermann's fairy tale industry is the beast that somehow endears itself to us.

These thoughts, however, come along later, after the photographs. When working, Rittermann thinks of people dear to him or of something that happened during the day. At night, wandering around, something will strike out at him, most often a sound. A deep hum. A whirr. Just inside the gate humanity dwells.

House, patch of meadow, oh evening light
Suddenly you acquire an almost human face
You are very near us, embracing and embraced.
                                        (Rilke)

Philipp Scholz Rittermann made these photographs in
harbor areas, at the edges of cities, and in industrial zones
in West Germany, Spain, France, and the United States
from 1980 to 1982.

The Women of Maciel

Photographs and text by Rio Branco

My interest in photographing prostitution areas in Brazil began in 1976 with an assignment in Brasilia and its satellite cities. I arrived in Luziania, a small town that had a *zona*—an area inhabited by prostitutes. It was then I started making pictures of *zonas* in different Brazilian towns. My purpose was to convey the feeling of that special class of exploited women who did not know, it seemed, what was happening to them. The mood of these early pictures was very much a mixture of sensuality and drama. But I did not truly capture what I was looking for until I went to live in Salvador and came to know the Maciel community in the historic Pelourinho area of the city.

Something very special struck me as I came to know Maciel. It was the melding of the decay of the area with the scars of the people who live within its wretched walls. I went into the *zona* two and three times a week, making portraits of the people there, which gave me passage into hell. I tried to be part of the people in a way that would result in a strongly emotional and at the same time aesthetically expressive statement. It took me six months to penetrate the core of Maciel that to the outsider remains invisible. In the end it was crude almost to the point of being unbearable.

The community of Maciel is a tear in the social fabric of Salvador. Salvador was the first capital of Brazil, when it was a colony of Portugal and in full bloom. It remained so until the capital was moved to Rio de Janeiro in 1763. Salvador is situated on a 750-mile coastline that attracts a healthy and growing tourist population. It is a situation one finds throughout the tropical lands—a tourist trade that aggravates social tensions in a country where the social dissonance is already severe.

Salvador is considered the most Africanized city in the country. It drew its colonial wealth largely from sugar and cacao plantations, which were worked by 15 million African slaves imported after 1538. Its churches were among the most luxurious and beautiful, heavily decorated with gold and precious stones. In the center of town, two of the wealthiest churches, the cathedrals of Terreiro de Jesus and Saint Francis, mark the once opulent neighborhood of Pelourinho. It was here that the elite of Bahia, the Brazilian state, resided.

Of course, the tourist population has no memory—is often intentionally amnesiac—and the businesses that cater to it does not wish to express the truth of Pelourinho. But while tourists and other outsiders gaze at the large houses and the vestiges of former wealth, many Brazilians are reminded more of torture.

The word *pelourinho* refers to a stone column to which slaves were tied and publicly whipped. The column that stood in this area of Salvador has since been torn down, and in its place, provided by funds from UNESCO, stands a meaningless albeit colorful construction that, to outsiders, looks like a stage setting; but anyone who wanders away from the main street and into the side alleys penetrates the living tragedy of Maciel.

Maciel looks as if it has been ravaged by war. Families huddle in ruins, cold and suffering with the diseases that crawl the walls. Street fighting is a daily recurrence. Pimps and old hags fight over the ownership of young prostitutes. Hundreds of abandoned children survive here, along with the old historic buildings that are left to decay and crumble into ruin. Summer fires and winter storms have caved in the roofs, but the people stay on. The authorities of Salvador, in order to make a good impression, want to relocate the inhabitants, but to do so would require force, and that would cause a public outcry. So the neighborhood, condemned to extinction, falls in on itself.

The marks of property cannot be mistaken here. Young bodies are heavily scarred from fights, torture, and syphilis and other diseases. Flashing switchblades slice through the flesh of those who do not observe the chain of command. Terezão da Lapo has her own identification mark, a half-moon scar between her young breasts, the result of burning coals carefully dropped there by the police. Adorinha had a swallow delicately scratched into her face by a razor blade while she was in prison for the murder of a friend. And there is Leninha, a novice in the trade, with cigar burns between her legs.

Today's Brazil wants to convince itself, and convince the world, that it is on the road to democratization. The Pelourinho Foundation, which is responsible for the reconstruction of the Pelourinho neighborhood, is providing a program for the social survival of the inhabitants of Maciel, but it is clearly perfunctory—a propaganda maneuver by the government. The uncontrollable violence in Maciel will not go away with enforced curfews or even with the infusion of massive social aid.

In these streets cluttered with brothels and bars, many of the buildings belong to the Church. In them is life without hope. The sounds of Brazilian blues mingled with African percussion are outward signs of life, trying to push back the horrors of survival. But on the wall of a stairwell in a brothel is the inscription: *I will take nothing with me when I die. Those who owe me debts will pay them in HELL.*

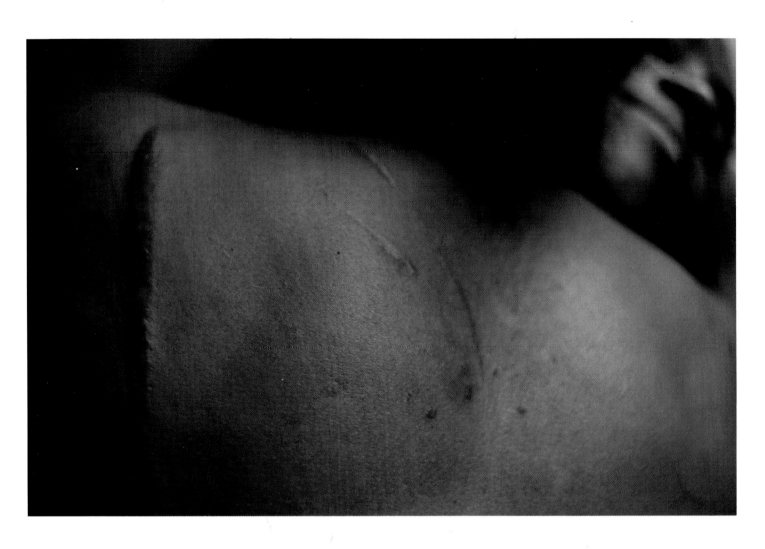

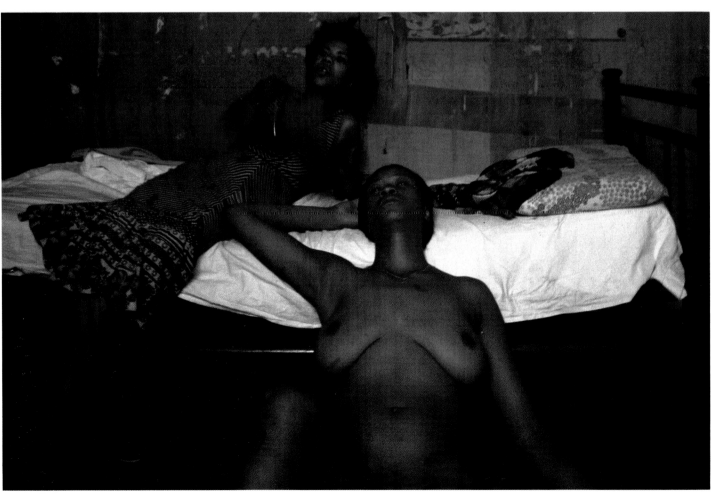

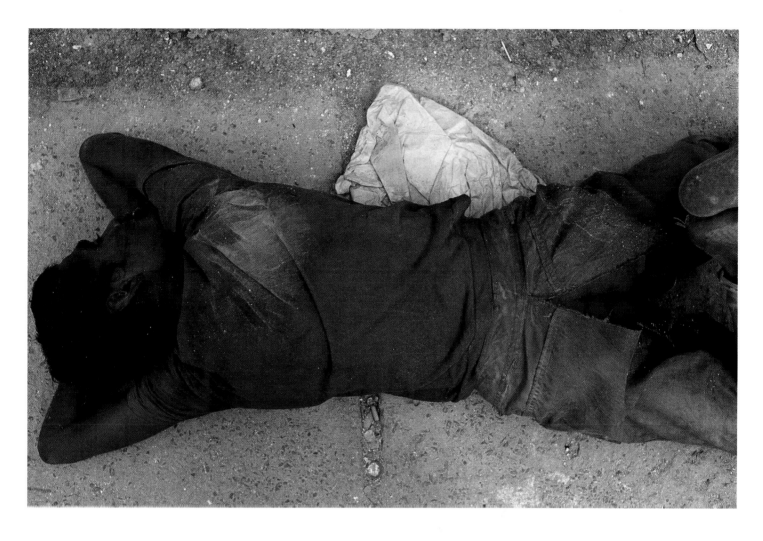

These photographs of the Maciel community in Salvador, Bahia, in northwestern Brazil, were made in 1976.

LABERINTO

No habrá nunca una puerta. Estás adentro
y el alcázar abarca el universo
y no tiene ni anverso ni reverso
ni externo muro ni secreto centro.
No esperes que el rigor de tu camino
que tercamente se bifurca en otro,
que tercamente se bifurca en otro,
tendrá fin. Es de hierro tu destino
como tu juez. No aguardes la embestida
del toro que es un hombre y cuya extraña
forma plural da horror a la maraña
de interminable piedra entretejida.
No existe. Nada esperes. Ni siquiera
en el negro crepúsculo la fiera.

JORGE LUIS BORGES

LABYRINTH

There'll never be a door. You're inside
and the keep encompasses the world
and has neither obverse nor reverse
nor circling wall nor secret center.
Hope not that the straitness of your path
that stubbornly branches off in two,
and stubbornly branches off in two,
will have an end. Your fate is ironbound,
as is your judge. Forget the onslaught
of the bull that is a man and whose
strange and plural form haunts the tangle
of unending interwoven stone.
He does not exist. In the black dusk
hope not even for the savage beast.

Ralston Crawford's Gift of Selection

By John Heilpern

Ralston Crawford's paintings of the 1930s and '40s of the newly exploding American industrial landscape firmly established him as one of the finest artist-poets of modern technology. Yet his photographs, some ten thousand images that involved him deeply and consistently for more than thirty years, are little known. Exhibitions and publications of the photographs have been seen infrequently in the United States. Crawford apparently did little during his lifetime to encourage widespread interest in them. The director of the Sheldon Art Gallery in Lincoln, Nebraska (which mounted an exhibition of Crawford photographs in 1974), wrote with a hint of exasperation: "Few artists have so little sought the attention of the public."

Now that a major exhibition of Crawford pictures has been assembled, originating in March 1983 at the University of Maryland Art Gallery (together with a sixty-page catalogue) and moving to the Frederick S. Wight Art Gallery at U.C.L.A. in September, many viewers are discovering an added dimension to Crawford's reflective and disciplined art.

In fact, this dimension—Crawford's photographs—was recognized more than thirty years ago by an early Crawford champion, James Johnson Sweeney, and his fine introduction to a 1950 exhibition of Crawford's paintings, prints, and photographs, in New Orleans, is unlikely to be bettered:

"What characterizes this harmony that gives Crawford's work the individuality we recognize throughout—even in such widely different media as photography and oil painting?

"Perhaps the term 'visual understatement,' if one may be permitted to use it, would provide the more suggestive description. Nothing overstressed. The eye never sated. The onlooker is always left with an appetite for just a slightly warmer tone, for a stronger, more emphatic line. Still each of these minor understatements is related to other understatements throughout the canvas: an avoidance of compositional crowding that balances on the verge of emptiness—an emphasis on perspective lines that never bore a hole into the picture's surface. . . . In all Crawford's best work we have this provision of subtle, delicate tensions. From the homely materials from which he derives the suggestions for his pictures, we are led to expect a banal and lifeless effect; and we are always surprised by the atmosphere of unfamiliarity he gives the eventual outcome through his understatement, this elimination of certain details—this selection.

"The result, this signature we spoke of that marks all his fully realized paintings, graphic work, and photographs—the basic aim of his selective approach is a cool, unworldly, or, perhaps more exactly, otherworldly calm. Not a haunted, paralyzed dream calm such as that in the empty perspective of

Maitland Bridge #2, 1938, oil on canvas

Giorgio de Chirico, nor the sultry calm of saturated color in Léger's strong, simple compositions, nor the warm intensity of Mondrian's: but a quiet, reticent, lyric ease. In fact, the final picture is often more reminiscent of the movement and shapes of water plants in a pool than of the harsh, forbidding contours of industrial forms out of which Crawford's pictures have ostensibly sprung."

Sweeney was right to link Crawford's paintings directly to his photographs. (And how could they not link? They have the same eye in common.) They share the same "quiet, reticent, lyric ease," a similar abstraction, and identical themes in terms of America's industrial icons—water tanks, factories, bridges, ships, and steel mills, the silhouettes and shapes of modern America.

It is also clear that Crawford used and valued photography for its own sake. There were times when his photographs were the equivalent of a note or a sketch; other times they were the source and inspiration of a painting. "My photography follows my painting in a great measure," he wrote in his unpretentious way in a 1949 issue of *Modern Photography*. So it is in general of a rather abstract variety. To be sure, there is some interaction. A few years ago, the idea of working from photographs was considered "inartistic." Now many painters recognize photographs as an informative, stimulating source to be incorporated into their work along with other experience.

Crawford also saw photography as freeing the painter. He felt that photography did not narrow the artist's vision but broadened it. There was no internal debate along the often neurotic lines of art versus photography. (He was a sensible man.) On the contrary, Crawford embraced the camera. He carried a camera wherever he went, just in case.

At the same time, the photograph itself was what he was after. He often returned to photograph a subject long after he had painted it—a favorite bridge or a New Orleans graveyard perhaps—sometimes over and over again throughout his life, as if obssessed by the possibilities of reality and image. There were also photographic themes, particularly a crucial aspect of his work—his pictures of New Orleans jazz musicians—that he never painted.

But whether or not a Crawford photograph became a painting or was linked to a painting, that photograph exists in its own right.

Both as photographer and as painter, Ralston Crawford received what Charles Sheeler termed the Good Housekeeping "seal of approval." Along with Sheeler and others, Crawford became known as a Precisionist. Broadly speaking, the Precisionist school lumped together artists such as Sheeler, Georgia O'Keeffe, Niles Spencer, Stuart Davis, and Crawford, who reflected a common interest in a more precise and simplified art whose primary interest was machine-age America.

Unlike the European schools of the day—the German Bauhaus, Russian Constructivism, Dutch De Stijl—the Precisionists issued no group manifestos. But they reflected the "machine aesthetic" of Europe, adapting it to their own American needs. Crawford, like Milton Avery and Arthur Dove, was in his own way bringing the new abstract and Cubist forms from Europe into American realism. Karen Tsujimoto points out in *Images of America—Precisionist Painting and Modern Photography* (1983) that, as with Niles Spencer, Crawford's formative roots were in the work of Cézanne and the Cubists, particularly Picasso and Gris, whose paintings he knew from his studies at the Barnes Foundation in Merion, Pennsylvania, and from his travels in Europe in the early 1930s.

At the same time, photographers of the period such as Paul

Strand, Walker Evans, Berenice Abbott, Ralph Steiner, and Edward Weston were also responding to the radical changes that were transforming America in the 1920s and '30s. "I am fascinated by man's work and the civilization he's built," said Walker Evans. "In fact, I think that's *the* interesting thing in the world—what man does."

Crawford, who was familiar with Evans's work, was like many of his contemporaries absorbed by the new geometric shapes and structures of contemporary America. Viewed from his perspective, they also reflected his interest in abstract realism. All of Crawford's photographs and paintings are rooted in reality, in objects found and observed. (They also have literal titles—a point of reference.) But the form itself evolved from reduction and abstraction, as did Paul Strand's photographs, which Crawford greatly admired. "My pictures mean exactly what they say," Crawford once explained. "And what they say is said in color and shapes." He also said about all of his work: "I have invented very little. I have selected and reordered and recombined."

You cannot look at a Crawford photograph without sensing this gift so evident in all his work—what James Johnson Sweeney called "his gift of selection"—of choices made and of compositions carefully fashioned not haphazardly but in stillness and quiet, with great clarity and control.

He was, as Richard B. Freeman, an early Crawford champion, described him, "an observer-commentator." A Crawford photograph, whether it be the rig of a fishing boat, vases at the base of a grave, the architecture of an elevated subway, a jar and wires, a bridge, can appear coolly mathematical in its composition. In a 1953 lecture, Crawford quoted, surprisingly, the great turn-of-the-century mathematician Henri Poincaré, who delivered a lecture on mathematical creation before the Psychological Society in Paris. "Had it been written by an artist,"

Women in Front of Barber Shop, New Orleans, 1960

said Crawford, "I think it might have been rejected as vague dreaming by nearly all but artists."

He then quoted briefly from Poincaré's lecture: "It might be surprising to see an emotional sensibility invoked apropos of

Bill Mathews #6 (New Orleans), 1950

mathematical demonstrations that, it would seem, can interest only the intellect. This would be to forget the feeling of mathematical beauty, of the harmony of numbers and forms, of geometric elegance. This is a true aesthetic feeling that all mathematicians know, and it surely belongs to emotional sensibility."

In the Crawford photographs that relate most directly to his paintings—the Maitland Bridge series, the boats, the St. Louis Cemetery pictures, for example—can be found this mathematical precision and symmetry. Yet they are not cold pictures: in their own way, they are emotionally charged. There is a sense of wonder within them at man-made America. Other photographers concentrated on the people who crossed the bridges or who traveled on the Third Avenue El. Crawford took us inside the structures and the machinery. He didn't romanticize them. Nor did he simply and objectively record them. Better than that, he helped to define and redefine them for us.

He was concerned with what he phrased "the properties of the twentieth century." But in sometimes startling contrast to his nonfigurative paintings, his photographs also moved in another direction. Abstract realism is not always predominant. At first sight, particularly in the jazz-musician series, it is as if the pictures might have been made by another artist.

Crawford, a highly independent man, a cultured bohemian, traveled all his life. He was born in 1906 in Ontario, but New York became his base. At twenty, he became a sailor on tramp steamers, which took him to the Caribbean and Central America and to California, where he began his art studies. He was the son of a ship's captain. The sea, movement, travel were essential to him: a form of lifeblood.

Over the years, Crawford traveled through America, teaching in more than a dozen schools and university departments. He carried his camera to New Orleans, Mexico, Spain, Egypt, France, Scandinavia, North Africa, Ireland, and Scotland. He worked on Tobago and Trinidad, on Guadeloupe and Martinique, on the Isle of Man, in the Orkney and Shetland islands and the Outer Hebrides, and in the South Pacific. The islands gave him isolation. The bullrings in Mexico City and in Spain, the racecourses at Le Mans, the jazz clubs of New Orleans were photographed, too, and with marvelous results.

Crawford was attracted to the pagan ritual of the bullrings almost as much as he was to George Lewis and his clarinet in New Orleans. His other interest—Grand Prix racing—also mirrored an important part of his own character. An admiration for control, audacity, tension and skill, sensuality of form. The bullfight is a ritual not only of life and death but of dignity and precision. All—the matador, the racing-car driver, the jazz musician—improvise, as the artist does. All share at least this in common with Crawford: they are virtuoso performers.

New Orleans was Crawford's first love. (He chose to be buried there.) From the 1940s until his death in 1978, he chronicled the bars and buildings, above all the jazzmen and singers and families, flamboyant and sad in small back rooms. The results are deeply humanizing images of what he described as the "broad, profound, social expression" of New Orleans.

They are a unique record, as are his hundreds of photographs—also taken obsessively throughout his life—of St. Louis Cemetery, still-life abstractions pervaded by decay and timelessness at the same time: "other reality."

Crawford collected jazz records; he took photographs for albums, posters, and programs; he illustrated small New Orleans jazz journals; his notebooks—he never threw anything away, from matchbooks to hotel notepaper—are of musicians' addresses, names of people to be photographed, dates of jam sessions and parades, snatches of conversations, lyrics of songs. All are noted down methodically in childlike capital letters.

The people of New Orleans must have trusted and liked him. The jazz musicians invited him into their homes and to their parties. They accepted him completely and were his friends. Yet Crawford himself seems more of an outsider than the photographs and his warm relationship with New Orleans suggest.

One of his three sons, Neelon Crawford, an experimental film maker, once filmed his father painting in his Manhattan studio. The image of Crawford, Sr., who was then sixty-five, is unexpected: it is as if a fastidious, successful Wall Street banker had taken up art. He was dressed for the office, wearing a custom-made suit, an image of sobriety, as he painted a canvas with firm manicured hands. He liked tailored suits and custom-made shirts just as he enjoyed fine wines. His suspenders, however, were yellow.

"He was an interesting character," Neelon says with obvious affection. "He was outwardly correct, a combination of humility and arrogance. I thought he was wonderful. He wasn't good at playing softball with me when I was eight, but he taught me

Test Able, 1946, oil on canvas

a lot. I often went with him on his travels. He really did live life fully and sought it out aggressively. He was never side-tracked. He was a rooted person. He was awake and searching and very focused on what he wanted to accomplish. He was a feisty character."

The point about Crawford is that in all his pursuits—photography, painting, drawing, and lithography—he accomplished what he set out to do. He was fully engaged in each medium, using each for its own particular ends. It is significant that when, in 1946, he was the only artist to witness Test Able, the detonation of an atomic bomb on Bikini, he chose not to photograph it. The experience changed him deeply, however, and he painted it.

The photographic images of the atomic explosion were made familiar through the press. When Crawford removed his pro-

tective glasses to witness the explosion with his naked eye, thereby risking blindness, his instinct was to turn to the medium of expression that could reflect his shattered feelings, which documentary photography could not.

From then on, Crawford's paintings changed dramatically and departed from his photographs. As Freeman pointed out, gone were the classic line, the monumental design, and the restrained palette of his earlier paintings. In their place, form itself exploded and splintered into purer abstraction. The photographs, on the other hand, continued for the most part in the more literal form of abstract reality and that "quiet, reticent, lyric ease" of his earlier paintings, described by Sweeney.

It is arguable that Crawford accepted the more traditional limitations in photography that he did not accept in painting. Perhaps he saw greater possibilities in painting. Perhaps photography fulfilled what he had to say in the form. But he kept taking photographs, reworking and reexamining his familiar themes, until he died.

Neelon Crawford showed me two short silent films made by his father in the late 1960s. (He had made films since the 1940s, but they are scarcely known.) The first, "Various Depths," projects certain images for several minutes at a time: a rope attached to a boat, which changes perspective as the boat moves in the water; neon lights; traffic at night in the big city; a stationary racing car; a car race, a blur; the exterior of a cathedral.

The second film contains prolonged seductive images of a torn billboard; a transparent curtain blown by a draft; a calm, ghostly Big Bayou Black River swamp in Mississippi; a woman's face; a motorcycle mirror reflecting the sky; Crawford himself riding off on the motorcycle.

The short films take his paintings and photographs further. He used film to explore movement itself. A torn poster and a transparent curtain have an apparent life: they can move. The Precisionist in Crawford was content to focus on these images for minutes, or hours, to see reality. The hypnotic images relate directly to the paintings and photographs he began in the 1930s and continued until the 1970s. All the forms and sources link the essentials, which is the shape and mystery of physical reality.

Crawford died at the age of seventy-one, en route to New Orleans. His will requested that he be buried in St. Louis Cemetery, which he had photographed so often. He had a jazz funeral, one of the few white men to be given one. I have the feeling he enjoyed it.

Ralston Crawford Photographs/Art and Process, by Edith A. Tonelli and John Gossage, is the catalogue for the exhibition of Ralston Crawford's pictures that originated at the University of Maryland Art Gallery in March 1983 and traveled to the Frederick S. Wight Art Gallery at U.C.L.A., September 27–November 13, 1983. The catalogue is available from the Art Gallery, University of Maryland, College Park, Maryland.

Pamplona, 1970

Third Avenue Elevated Platform, New York City, n.d.

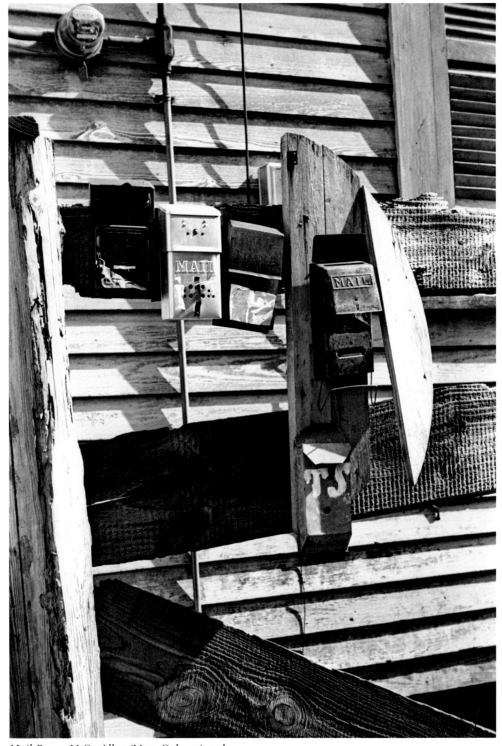

Mail Boxes N.O. Alley (New Orleans), n.d.

Third Avenue Elevated Platform, New York City, 1948

Door, 1954

New Orleans Building Façade, about 1966

David Haxton, *Squares in Magenta and Orange*, 1982

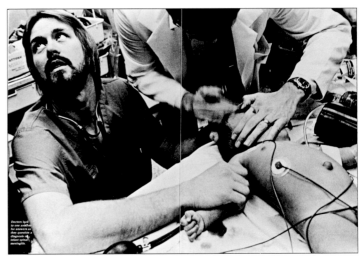

Eugene Richards, from "Vital Signs," 1983

People and Ideas

(continued from page 5)

So much for the influence on public opinion for which I had worked so hard. Most of the public would never see these books, which were done as alternative photo essays to the pabulum then being served up by *Life* and *Look* magazines in the 1960s.

Public opinion no longer controls the running of America. We have lost our democracy, mostly through lack of courage. That was ultimately *Camera Arts'* finest quality and its fatal flaw. The magazine exhibited courage. In a world that nourishes mediocrity, it tried to be bold. Dziga Vertov, the great Russian documentary film maker, said, "Unity of form and content guarantees success." In this sad time, with our powers usurped, aesthetic success guarantees failure.

If in 1963 a twenty-year-old woman in the Student Nonviolent Coordinating Committee (SNCC) was able to make and circulate a filmstrip of atrocities being committed by American soldiers in Vietnam, then why couldn't CBS? By the time CBS and the rest of the media joined the bandwagon of opposition to the war, it was too late. Our nation was stuck deep in the mud of an American tragedy from which it has barely begun to recover. In 1964 when a strong and honest stand on the war could have effectively alerted the public, *Look* magazine ran prowar articles with full-page color spreads of U.S. marines sloshing through rice paddies defending America from an unseen menace. When the My Lai massacre occurred the *New York Times* ran a front-page story about a great victory by the Americal division. Two years later it finally corrected itself. In our democracy it was the most grave responsibility of Walter Cronkite, *Look* magazine, and the *New York Times* to deliver to us the truth. And how miserably they failed.

Is America a free country? Are we a free people? *If* we are then why does our government do things that most of us oppose? Hitlerian concepts are now pursued by the United States in El Salvador, Nicaragua, and Guatemala, resulting in

TESTING ANSEL ADAMS' TECHNIQUES

Camera Arts

July 1983 $2.95

ANTHONY BARBOZA
HUGH BELL
HARRY CALLAHAN
ROY DECARAVA
LARRY FINK
LEE FRIEDLANDER
WILLIAM GOTTLIEB
GJON MILI
JAY MAISEL
MAN RAY
BRUNO STEVENS
DENNIS STOCK

Cover of the Final Issue; *Hamiet Blueitt* by Anthony Barboza

real war suffering and immense human upheaval. Living in America has become more and more difficult. Our cities and countryside have been virtually destroyed by government and corporate decisions or neglect.

Our country is so constructed that the television and the press are central to the functioning of our democracy. Unfortunately, the founding fathers could not have envisioned CBS or Ziff-Davis. Access by serious minds and alternative views to the American people has always been fundamental to making our democracy work. That access no longer exists. All of television is closed to serious-minded people. The aesthetics of the Public Broadcasting System exclude all film makers who do not share its point of view. It is as if a series of great screens were set up so that any artist or idea must pass through each one before coming out the other end in twenty million living rooms. The screens are so set that only junk comes out the bottom. Anything of quality, anything of power, is excluded.

Malcolm X, who was as radical as Abraham Lincoln, talked of "the ballot or the bullet." We have the power to change things, but we are too dazed to use it. The media feed us the pabulum we seem to enjoy. We gulp it down. Luis Buñuel argued that the public gets what it deserves. Perhaps, but I wonder if the deck hasn't been stacked against us.

Who killed *Camera Arts*? I hate to admit it, but probably we did.

DANNY LYON

CONTRIBUTORS

Mark Haworth-Booth

Mark Haworth-Booth is assistant keeper of photographs at the Victoria and Albert Museum, London. He has organized numerous exhibitions of photography, including one-man shows of Don McCullin and Henri Cartier-Bresson. He is now preparing *The Golden Age of British Photography, 1839–1900*, an exhibition that will tour the United States in 1984. The accompanying publication will be published by Aperture.

Philipp Scholz Rittermann

Born in Lima, Peru, Philipp Scholz Rittermann is presently working at the Center for Photographic Arts in San Diego. He has exhibited extensively in Europe, where he lived from 1969 until 1982. His photographs have appeared in *Camera*, *European Photography*, and *Photo Metro*.

Ralston Crawford

Ralston Crawford's paintings and lithographs are included in the permanent collections of America's major museums. During his highly creative life, Crawford also made some ten thousand photographs, beginning in 1938 with a study of a prison camp in Orlando, Florida. He died in 1978.

Ben Maddow

Ben Maddow is a writer and director whose poems, short stories, plays, and films have received numerous international awards. He has had a lifelong interest in photography and photographers.

Danny Lyon

A photographer and film maker for over twenty years, Danny Lyon has most recently published *Pictures from the New World* (Aperture, 1981), a survey of his photographs since 1962.

Rio Branco

Rio Branco was born in Brazil, where he began his career as a painter, later freelancing as a commercial photographer and film maker. In 1970 he moved to New York, pursuing documentary photography and experimental film making for the following three years. In São Paulo, he received the Grand Prix of Triennale in photography. His film, *Napa*, earned the best prize for cinematography at the Brasilia Film Festival. Rio Branco is affiliated with Magnum Photos.

Markéta Luskačová

Born in Czechoslovakia and educated as a sociologist and journalist, Markéta Luskačová first made photographs to illustrate her academic work on traditional religion. She later attended the Academy of Film Arts, Prague, and freelanced for Theater Behind the Gate and for *Zdravi* (Czech Red Cross) magazine before emigrating to Britain. Since 1975 she has worked as a freelance photographer based in London. Luskačová received Arts Council of Great Britain Awards in 1975 and 1976. An exhibition of her photographs will open at the Victoria and Albert in 1984.

Mary Wachs

Mary Wachs is managing editor of *Aperture*.

WILLIAM · CHRISTENBERRY

SOUTHERN PHOTOGRAPHS · LIMITED EDITION

HOUSE AND CAR, NEAR AKRON, ALABAMA, 1981

William Christenberry's photographs of the red clay hills of Hale County, Alabama—his native
territory—were presented in the volume *Southern Photographs,* which Walker Percy proclaimed
"a poetic evocation of a haunted countryside." Praising the photographs of this major American artist,
Walker Evans noted their "quiet honesty, subtlety, restrained strength and refreshing purity."

Aperture proudly offers to its subscribers a deluxe edition of *Southern Photographs*
limited to 100 numbered and signed copies. Each volume is handsomely bound
and slipcased, and accompanied by an original Ektacolor print, *House and Car,
near Akron, Alabama, 1981* (image 8 × 10 inches), signed by the photographer.
The print is mounted on archival board and presented in a special folio.

The limited edition is $300.00

APERTURE, Millerton, New York 12546   (518) 789-4491

Lee Friedlander

Portraits October 18–November 12, 1983 New York

Lee Friedlander, The Estate of Paul Strand, and Harry Callahan
are represented by Zabriskie

Lee Friedlander, *Paul Tate, 1968*

Paul Strand

New York October 20–November 12, 1983

Mexican Photographs and
Photogravures of the 1930s

ZABRISKIE

724 Fifth Avenue, New York 10019. Tel. 307-7430
37 Rue Quincampoix, 75004, Paris. Tel. 272-3547